PERSONALITIES

IN

AMERICAN ART

PERSONALITIES

IN

AMERICAN ART

BY

WILLIAM FRANCKLYN PARIS

Essay Index Reprint Series

BOOKS FOR LIBRARIES PRESS
FREEPORT, NEW YORK

First Published 1930
Reprinted 1970

STANDARD BOOK NUMBER:
8369-1582-8

LIBRARY OF CONGRESS CATALOG CARD NUMBER:
72-107731

PRINTED IN THE UNITED STATES OF AMERICA

CONTENTS

Foreword

*I*N one of his lectures on "Heroes and Hero Worship," Carlyle sets down as a verity that "Great Men are profitable company." In a lifetime spent in the study and practice of the "Beaux Arts" it has been my good fortune to approach and know a number of artists whom a hurrying world stopped long enough to label "great" and because they had proved to me the most valuable company, spiritually, I used what feeble talents I possessed to trumpet their glory and chronicle their fame.

Here are assembled a few rhetorical posies laid on the altars of James McNeill Whistler, Lloyd Warren, Egerton Swartwout, J. Sanford Saltus, Augustus Saint Gaudens, Clinton Ogilvie, Samuel F. B. Morse, and William M. Chase.

In my capacity as Director of the Hall of Remembrance of New York University I was instrumental in placing the busts of Whistler, Saint Gaudens, Ogilvie, Morse and Chase in this pantheon for artists in the rotunda of the university's library where I also installed busts of Carroll Beckwith, Walter Shirlaw, Frank Duveneck, J. Q. A. Ward, Henry K. Brown and George Inness.

These men were my seniors and these eulogies of them represent my enthusiasms and sometimes my personal attachment and affection. The opinions I have voiced as to the genius or artistic talent of each of them are, I believe, just and not the encomiums of a prejudiced partisan. I studied under Chase, worked with Egerton Swartwout and played with Saltus. Lloyd Warren I knew through the eyes of his distinguished brother, Whitney Warren, and Clinton Ogilvie was revealed to me through the heart of his inconsolable widow.

I could have added to my list of "Great Artists Whom I Have Known" the biographies of several who outrank in artistic genius and accomplishment the eight assembled in this tribute, but the reader will note that I sing the man rather than the artist in these sketches and that those I bring into the light are nearly all of a modest and retiring spirit, or crusaders battling for an ideal and scorning popularity. The fighter makes enemies and the timid man stays in the shadow. They need apologists. The assertive and the gregarious press-agent themselves or belong to coteries which herald their fame in and out of reason. They need no champion.

A charming society philosopher of the Victorian era, Madame Emile de Girardin, observed in one of her spirituelles "Lettres Parisiennes" that it was sad but true that in the present day world, one achieved quicker and greater

success *through one's defects than through one's qualities.*
To be conscious of one's limitations was fatal to success.
To be confident to the point of pretentiousness was on the
contrary to command success, on the theory that if you
think well of yourself, others will think well of you.

The men whom I have memorialized in this volume habit-
ually did not think well of themselves. They conscientiously
strove to the utmost of their strength to reach an ideal and
because that ideal was very high they did not always at-
tain it. But must praise be given solely to those who win
the race and opprobrium fall on those who fail, irrespective
of the relative strength expended or effort exerted? "Before
censuring the captain who brings his ship into harbor with
battered hull and shrouds and tackle damaged, first tell
us," says Carlyle, "whether his voyage has been round the
globe or only to Ramsgate and the Isle of Dogs."

As artists, J. Sanford Saltus and Lloyd Warren did
not rank very high, but no artist of my day and generation
exceeded them in their zeal for art and their inspiriting
efforts in behalf of young artists. The Beaux Arts Insti-
tute of Design remains as a monument to Lloyd Warren
and had not death suddenly and unexpectedly ended the
days of Sanford Saltus, the School of Arts of New York
University would stand today as material evidence of Mr.
Saltus' interest in Art. As far back as 1920 I suggested to
him the endowment of a chair for the instruction of the

Fine Arts at New York University and he seized upon the suggestion with eagerness. I had gone as far as to propose a donation of $75,000. towards this end to Chancellor Brown of the university when death put an end to the negotiations. I am sure that had Mr. Saltus lived his donations to the Art Department of the university would have been many times the $75,000. originally offered.

The seed planted in 1920 has borne fruit and the Fine Arts Department of New York University is an established fact through the generosity of another art patron, Col. Michael Friedsam. I like to think, however, that but for Mr. Saltus' and my own feeble efforts the University's long dead School of the Fine Arts might have waited another decade or two before being revived.

JAMES McNEILL WHISTLER
Edmond T. Quinn, *Sculptor*

JAMES McNEILL WHISTLER

IN his celebrated lecture, "Ten O'Clock," delivered in London in the Spring of 1885, Whistler traced the emergence of the first-artist. "In the beginning," said he, "men went forth each day, some to do battle, some to the chase, others again to dig and to delve in the field, all that they might gain and live, or lose and die, until there was found among them, differing from the rest, one whom these pursuits attracted not, and so he stayed by the tents with the women and traced strange devices with a burnt stick upon a gourd. This man, who took no joy in the ways of his brethren, who cared not for conquest and fretted in the field, who perceived in nature about him curious carvings, as faces are seen in the fire, this dreamer apart, was the first artist."

I only met Whistler once and I retain from the meeting only a memory of his physical appearance. It was in Paris, in 1900, when he no longer was the musketeer and dandy, but a little old man, with thick curly gray hair and a lively sparkle in his keen blue eyes darting from under shaggy and bristling eyebrows. That meeting gave me little occasion to appraise his character or analyze his temperament. I was a mere boy in the presence of Genius and I was tongue-tied and overawed. But in many conversations with my good friend, the lamented Joseph Pennell, who was as a brother to Whistler, I got to know Whistler spiritually and I see in this description of the first artist a self-portrait in which he paints himself as he was, "a man who took no joy in the ways of his brethren," a dreamer apart, who saw in the fire faces not seen by other eyes.

I speak to you today in the place of Joseph Pennell who would have delivered, had he been here to do so, a better and more eloquent tribute to "Jamie" than my limited powers will permit. I thank Mrs. Pennell for honoring us with her presence on this occasion. She, too, knew Whistler well and loved him in spite of his many faults associated with genius and the artistic temperament. Mr. E. G. Kennedy is also here, "O. K." as Whistler affectionately called him, and he, too, could have given you a better eulogy, but since the untimely taking off of the one and the self-effacing modesty of the other will not let them speak, you will have to endure the poor homage of one who speaks from hearsay only.

Oscar Wilde described Whistler as a "miniature

Mephistopheles mocking the majority," but I prefer to think of him as another Cyrano, the Cyrano of Rostand, a man constantly at war with Society, but at peace with his conscience, lashing the imbeciles with an almost cruel wit, but deep down in his soul a tenderhearted poet.

Who but a poet could have written the passage in this same "Ten O'clock" lecture depicting the coming of night along the Thames embankment, "when the evening mist clothes the riverside with poetry as with a veil, and the poor buildings lose themselves in the dim sky, and the tall chimneys become campanili, and the warehouses are palaces in the night, and the whole city hangs in the heavens, and fairyland is before us."

When I first conceived the idea of making this rotunda a Pantheon to American Artists, my first thought was of Whistler. I sought out Pennell and I found him enthusiastic over the idea, but all the support he could give me was moral. There were apparently no friends ready to contribute funds for the making and installing of a Whistler bust. Poor "Jamie" had been only too successful in "the gentle art of making enemies." There were plenty to concede his genius and his greatness but few to give financial evidence of their admiration or regard.

I found that lesser artists had left behind them kindlier memories, so I accepted and installed the tokens of love to Ward, Saint Gaudens, Ogilvie, Henry K. Brown, Innes, Carroll Beckwith, Duveneck, Chase and Shirlaw that you see enshrined between these columns.

Whistler lived most of his life in Paris and London. Although an American, educated at West Point with the idea of eventually serving as an officer in the American Army, Whistler was a citizen of the world. He was violent in his assertion that art has no nationality and it was in keeping with this sentiment that he created the International Society of Sculptors, Painters and Engravers. He was long President of this Society and not only Paris and London, but Dresden, Munich, Rome and Edinburgh acclaimed him long before his own country became aware of his greatness.

As a matter of fact, from his twenty-first birthday to his death he lived away from the United States and he lies buried in London. His art apprenticeship was spent in the Latin Quarter of Paris and his early and most lasting friendships were French and British. For a while he even nursed a grudge against the country of his birth for a fancied slight which he thought had been visited upon him by the American

officials in charge of the American Art Exhibit at
the International Exposition held in Paris in 1889.
He had sent two paintings and twenty-seven etchings to be shown in the American section of the Exposition but withdrew them all when he received
a curt letter from the Commissioner for the American Art Department saying; "Sir, ten of your exhibits have not received the approval of the jury.
Will you kindly remove them." That year Whistler
exhibited in the British section.

All this in a way explains the seeming indifference, the lack of personal following which I encountered when I first sought to obtain subscrip-
tions to a fund for a Whistler bust. I must say that
in 1920, when I first busied myself with this Memorial to American Artists I did not know Edward
G. Kennedy very well. As soon as circumstances
brought me in contact with this enlightened patron
of the arts and staunch friend of the great painter
whom we honor today, my perplexities were ended
and the success of the Whistler Memorial assured.
It can no longer be said, therefore, that a prophet is
not without honor, save in his own country.

Mr. Kennedy had already aided in making per-
manent the fame of Whistler by his publication
under the auspices of the Grolier Club of a monu-

mental catalogue of Whistler's etchings, and by the presentation to the Metropolitan Museum of Art of his own portrait by the great master. More recently he presented to the New York Public Library a collection of one hundred and thirty-five letters written to him by Whistler, and your Chairman, Mr. Cortissoz, may tell you of a new and unsuspected Whistler revealed by these letters. In one of the letters the militant and misunderstood artist pathetically expresses his joy at having a friend in his one-time patron. "A friend," he writes, "my dear Kennedy. A tried friend! I doubt if I shall know how to deal with him. I have no habit." Reflect a moment on this "I have no habit." Whistler coming out from behind his mask of impassiveness and disdain to confess that he is human and craves friendship but hasn't "the habit" of inspiring friendship. Poor "Jamie" admitting the disillusion and emptiness of his favorite avocation "the gentle art of making enemies."

Back in 1682 a French painter, Claude Gellée, known to the world at large as Claude Lorrain, was buried in Rome after many years of self-imposed exile from France, as Whistler is buried in London after many years of exile from his native land. On the tomb of this great artist is inscribed the sentiment that "the French nation does not forget her famous children even when they have died in foreign lands." This memorial in the Pantheon of American Artists may not be considered national in character, it is the expression of the sentiments of a relatively small group, but I like to believe that it voices the respect and admiration of the entire American nation for one of her most distinguished sons. Like the French nation, the American nation should remember her famous sons even when they have died in foreign lands. It should remember and honor Whistler in particular because living in foreign lands he has brought fame and prestige upon America in quarters where our renown is chiefly based upon our materialistic accomplishments. He has done for American Art what Poe and Fenimore Cooper did before him for American letters. Our physical exploits linger in European memories but in the realm of the spiritual we have few champions to uphold our standing as a cultured people.

Whistler was a superlative person. He had a positive horror of the commonplace and a fiery impatience for privilege and authority. He carried himself with an air of jaunty superiority and his lucent top hat, his monocle, his hands, almost justified the general belief that he was studiously eccentric and that the habit of his student days of doing everything possible to "épater le bourgeois" was too strong for him ever to overcome completely. He had humor, he had experience, he had "a petit air moqueur;" he was the last man in the world to be taken in. At the same time he had sensibilities. At the vulgar, the meretricious he shuddered; he would be sure to know pinchbeck from gold and to hate it.

It is not surprising that in the crowded world in which he moved he should have stepped on a few toes. His quarrel with Ruskin is famous. Ruskin had said that he "never expected to hear a coxcomb ask two hundred guineas for flinging a pot of paint in the public's face." The allusion was to Whistler's "Nocturne in Black and Gold," exhibited at the Grosvenor Gallery, and Whistler promptly sued, alleging libel and demanding a thousand pounds in damages. Although Whistler only obtained one farthing damages, the verdict was a vindication and Ruskin, feeling rebuked thereby, resigned as Fine Arts professor at Oxford.

The view of Ruskin that Whistler's art was "ill-educated conceit nearly approaching the aspect of willful imposture" and Burne-Jones' judgment that the Nocturne in question was only "one of the thousand failures to paint night" is proof of the truth voiced by Wordsworth that innovators have to create the taste by which they are to be admired. It is the destiny of artists who see nature in a novel manner to struggle for a long time against the incomprehension of the public. Rousseau, Corot, Millet and more recently, Manet, Degas, Claude Monet, Pisarro, Sisley, Renoir, Raffaelli and Gauguin were once regarded as violent radicals and dangerous revolutionists, all because, like Whistler, they were one and all enemies of conventionality. The judgment of art manifestations implies reference to a standard, but that standard changes and the radicals of yesterday are frequently the conservatives of today. Music is not simply melody and sometimes composers arrive at harmony by an agglomeration of dissonances. The art of Whistler is not simple; it is anything but photographic. As far back as 1863 a French critic had proclaimed him "le plus spirite des peintres." He was also "le plus spirituel." In everything he did, he was guided by the principle, enunciated by Poe, that "Art is the production of what the senses perceive in Nature through the veil of the soul." It is this soulful quality, apparent in all his works, that has retarded popularity. The public's attitude towards the subtle, the elusive, when not an attitude of torpid indifference, is an attitude of positive dislike. There is more in Whistler's paintings and etchings, particularly in his nocturnes, than is seen by the corporeal eye. The *profanum vulgus* saw in this idealistic art fantasmagoric evocations, laborious strivings for effect, and it is recorded that they laughed—may God forgive them—when they first beheld "The Little White Girl."

I think it was d'Annunzio who said of Lamartine "Quand on porte un Dieu en soi on le sait" (when one carries within himself a God, one is likely to be conscious of it). Whistler knew that he carried within him a spark of the sacred fire of genius and he was brutally blunt about asserting it, but it is opinion that crushes us and in spite of the indwelling consciousness of his superior nature, he suffered from the incomprehension of the public. His lofty contempt of the critics was largely put on to veil a sorely wounded susceptibility. The great man said to himself, "I will instruct my sorrow to be proud," and with jovial elegance and Louis Quatorzian grace he went his way, light o'glove and bright o'boot, apparently indifferent to the chorus of abuse and vituperation raised by his defiant disregard of the venerations of many centuries. His facile pen, his Voltairian wit, which he exercised with gusto at the expense of imbeciles irrespective of their social importance or influence, estranged him from men in high places who would have patronized him had he been of a nature to suffer patronage from anyone. He loved a *bon mot* and could not resist uttering one, even when it was barbed and carried with it the likelihood of wounding whomever it was aimed at.

He lived as he himself has said, "in surroundings of antagonism" and his sensitive nature suffered in consequence. Had he been more of a philosopher he would have found consolation in the thought that "age withers love, but not glory."

He tasted of Fame before his death, which is not given to all great artists. In 1892, France bestowed upon him the Legion of Honor and shortly thereafter he had the rare distinction, for a foreigner, of seeing his portrait of his mother hung in the Luxembourg, a purchase by the State. And yet, this bust is the first lasting expression by America of the recognition of his genius. Long before a memorial had been thought of in his own country a bust by Sir Edgar Boehm had been made in London and a monument by Rodin had been planned.

On the outside of the Pantheon in Paris is the inscription: "Aux Grands Hommes la Patrie Reconnaissante" (The Nation voices its gratitude to its

Great Men.) This Hall of Remembrance is not a National Pantheon, but let us hope that it does in a less degree for American Artists what the Pantheons of European capitals do for the great and the famous in all spheres of endeavor.

During the French Revolution, when a city had withstood a siege successfully, or an army fought well and victoriously, the Convention would decree that the fortress, or the army had "bien mérité de la Patrie," that is, had "deserved much from the Country." James McNeill Whistler not only has deserved much from his country, but he has deserved much from Art.

May his laurels lie easy on his brow!

LLOYD ELIOT WARREN
Frederick B. Clarke, *Sculptor*

LLOYD ELIOT WARREN *

"Who Nature and the Muses loved"

WHEN Ralph Waldo Emerson, speaking to the graduating class of Dartmouth College, urged upon the young manhood of the day not to renounce learning and romantic expectations to get land and money, place and name, he uttered the truth that the "domineering temper of this sensual world creates the extreme need of priests of science."

This was in 1838, and the sage of Concord had less grounds for alarm at the materialism of the age than he would have today, but what he said then was not wafted away on the summer breeze and lost. He is gone but his words remain. "The wintry blast of death kills not the buds of virtue. They spread beneath the beam of brighter suns through endless ages."

He warned his hearers that the vice of the times and of the country was an excessive pretension and he urged them to seek the shade and find wisdom in neglect. "Be content with a little light, so it be

*Reprinted by courtesy of Architectural Record.

your own," counseled the great American philosopher; "be neither chided nor flattered out of your
position of perpetual inquiry. Neither dogmatize
yourself, nor accept another's dogmatism and do
not renounce your right to traverse the star-lit des-
erts of truth for the premature comforts of an acre,
house and barn. Truth also has its roof, and bed and
board."

I was not familiar with this quotation until Lloyd
Warren brought it to my attention. I was chiding
him gently for his habit of self-effacement and this
was his justification and his defense. It paints the
man as well as anything I could say in praise of his
character, which was noble and sensitive and exquisite, and if there is any virtue in the saying "as
a man thinketh, so he is," then Lloyd Warren was
as Emerson would have wanted him to be.

He was born in Paris in 1868, so that his sympathy with the French point of view and his intimate
knowledge of the French character came to him by
right of inheritance, so to speak. Although educated
here, he returned to Paris upon his graduation from
the School of Arts and the School of Mines of Columbia University and enrolled as a student of the

École des Beaux Arts, where he remained six years. He always spoke of those six years as the happiest period in his life. The Latin Quarter of that day was no longer the Bohême of Murger, but the young men of the "Rive Gauche were still abreuvés d'idéal" and Lloyd Warren shared with them their contempt of the bourgeois and their belief that "il n'y a de vraiment beau que ce qui ne sert absolument à rien."

When he returned to this side he "went into business," but he was of a delicate nature and the miserable arithmetic of dollars and cents so offended his susceptibility that he gave it up in disgust.

> "The best of men have ever loved repose:
> They hate to mingle in the filthy fray,
> Where the soul sours, and gradual rancour grows
> Embittered more from peevish day to day."

Lloyd Warren was one of these, and rather than have his soul grow sour he gave up an easy career of a constructive architect and became a "priest of science."

He was convinced that the doctrines taught at the Beaux Arts were the only true religion, and he belonged to that little group of American students as the École who, sitting on the terrace of the Café Voltaire, on the Boul' Mich', back in 1890, had decided to form in New York a Beaux Arts Society, where the teachings of the institution in Rue Bonaparte might be brought within reach of such American students of Architecture as could not go to the mountain.

Many are the alumni of the École des Beaux Arts who have given of their funds and of their time to the Beaux Arts Society of New York, but not one has given as much of both as did Lloyd Warren. The New York institution was the only child of this soft-spoken and mild-mannered bachelor and he nursed it and favored it and was as proud of it as the mother of the Gracchi who rejoiced and gloried in her sons. Each year, when the time came to make up the inevitable deficit, and the list was being passed around for contributions to the relief fund, Lloyd Warren's name "led all the rest."

The Society of Beaux Arts Architects and the Beaux Arts Institute of Design, which it maintains at 304 East Forty-fourth Street, have lost in him the fairy godfather who could always be counted upon to come to the rescue when disaster threatened. It was he who paid off the mortgage on the building which the Society and the Institute occupied and again he who leaned over the shoulders of the students of the Institute and, in that kindly manner and low voice that stamped him as a courtly personage, corrected their errors or criticized their efforts.

In these criticisms never once did he yield to the temptation to indulge in sarcasm, never once did he move away from the work criticized without tempering the critique with some word of encouragement. He had borrowed the formula of Bonnat and generally greeted a drawing with the familiar "not bad . . . not good, but not bad" of that French master whom he loved and by whom he was highly esteemed. As a result, the young men of the Institute had a real affection for him as well as a high regard for his judgment and authority. Many of them he assisted financially and others he placed as draftsmen in his brother's office, or in other ateliers where his recommendation had weight.

He had secured for the students of the Institute the privilege, enjoyed by no other school of architecture or design, for graduates to whom had been

awarded the Institute's Prix de Paris to enter the
École des Beaux Arts without examination and last
year much of his time in Paris was spent in making
arrangements for a summer school of architecture to
be held at Fontainebleau.

He had an exquisite taste in all the finer arts and
it was a treat to hear him rail against Cubism,
Dadaism, Pointillism "and all that rot." He un-
bosomed himself to but few, however. His was a
reserved and squeamish personality, a fastidious being who "scorned adulation to receive or give."
When he conferred a grace he sought to make it
seem a debt paid to merit.

We were both active during the war, as members
of the Fraternité des Artistes, in coming to the assistance of the families of French painters and architects and to their widows and orphans. It was this
association that permitted me to penetrate his re-
serve and to see behind the mask of imperturbability
with which he veiled a highly sensitive nature. He
was a little ashamed, or at least terribly embarrassed
whenever any one perceived to what depth he was
stirred by his emotion. He loved the French and suffered agonies during the first weeks of the war, but

always he had the conviction that eventually right would prevail over might. "If I did not believe that," he told me, "life would hold nothing for me."

In his family life he was exemplary. His devotion to his parents and to two sisters, who died when he was just entering manhood, was of a quality that is no longer encountered. The relationship between him and his brother, Whitney Warren, was comparable to the classic friendship between Orestes and Pylades. The two were inseparable, and the same taste in music and art furnished occasion for as fine a companionship in ideas as is possible to conceive.

Although of a retiring disposition, Lloyd Warren held membership in many clubs—the Knickerbocker, the Union, Century Association, Racquet and Tennis, Tuxedo, Players, Automobile Club—but these castles of indolence saw less of him than his pupils of the Institute. He played a good game of tennis, played agreeably on the piano, enjoyed the play and the opera and "nothing human foreign was to him," but first of all he was Emerson's "priest of science," or of art, whose joy was in teaching.

In the funeral oration pronounced over his remains in St. Thomas' Church by the Rev. Dr. Mansfield, that distinguished divine spoke of the grace "that kindled in his heart deeds of friendliness and kindness, generous sacrifices and constant endeavor to serve his fellowmen in work and ways that have counted for good." *De mortuis nil nisi bonum*, and many are those over whom similar orations have been said. What distinguishes Lloyd Warren from the rest is that in this instance the eulogy was deserved.

As outward signs of his merit, he held the diploma of the French Government for Architecture, the Honorary Degree of Master of Arts conferred upon him last year by Yale University and the cross of the Legion of Honor given to him by France in recognition of his work in connection with the Fraternité des Artistes during the war.

"The wintry blast of death kills not the buds of virtue." The seed planted by Lloyd Warren has brought forth a harvest of fruit in the Beaux Arts Institute of Design which is yearly gaining in influence and prestige. The Institute is purely educational. Its funds are devoted absolutely and totally to educational purposes. Moreover, the money secured and expended is the least part of the value placed freely at the disposal of the public, for no salaries are paid to instructors.

The fact that the best men in architecture, sculpture, painting, and the decorative arts are glad to give their time freely to the Institute is proof of its high character. They are busy men whose services are in demand at the market price, but they know that the very life of their art, its place in the nation's development, depends on the kind of training which new recruits receive. They count it a privilege and honor to act as the guardians of a great tradition and to keep the fire of art burning on the altar of beauty. The fact that the Institute is freed from the care of having to provide material support for its instructors gives to its courses an element of freedom and flexibility absent in other educational organizations. Each instructor in turn gives his best and cheerfully makes way for another. The embarrassing situation of a superannuated mentor being retained because he needs the money never has to be faced.

Charlatans and self-advertisers are not tempted to intrude upon this quiet atmosphere of service. Indeed the students take such pride in the character of their school that pretence and false motives of any kind could not live there.

The Institute is the fully organized and altogether efficient thing which it is today because of the constant and unflagging interest and attention devoted to it in its formative period by Lloyd Warren. Few architects of the present generation have built themselves as stately a mansion.

EGERTON SWARTWOUT

EGERTON SWARTWOUT

"A seeing eye under an amused eyebrow"

IN one of his many brilliant articles on modern architecture Mr. Swartwout once emitted the apothegm that "one good church may, and often does, lead to another, and one good house, if it is well advertised, may lead to many, but one monumental building rarely leads anywhere."

Mr. Swartwout wields a facile pen and lovers of rationalism have applauded the accuracy of his aim when his shafts have been directed upon shams and formulas, the aberrations of cubism and futurism and the apostles of innovation. One surmises, however, that when he penned the quoted animadversion upon monumental buildings his tongue was in his cheek.

The generalization may be true, but it does not apply in his case, for instead of leading nowhere, one good monumental building has led to a better monumental building, until today he has to his credit a long line of public buildings, each more stately, more imposing, more beautiful than the last.

Mr. Swartwout's arrival on the summit which he now occupies proves the theory that "if you make love to a woman long enough, and ardently enough, you are sure to get rather fond of her at last.'' It may also prove that architects—that is good architects— are born and not made. He did not set out deliber- ately to make himself an architect, in the sense that he did not study in any architectural school, but he loved beauty instinctively and had a holy horror of the commonplace, and so when he found himself in an architect's office he did not remain a mere pencil pusher. He remained in that office a great many years and he made love to architecture a long, long time, and it was ardent love, for Mr. Swartwout is an assertive person, and finally he got rather fond of his art. According to Dionysius, there are nine orders of angels. With the highest, the Seraphim, knowledge springs from love. I do not know how Egerton Swartwout will like being compared to a Seraph, but it is true of him to say that his knowl- edge springs from love.

He loves beauty and he loves nature. Forever con- trasting the actual with the ideal, he is a Greek in spirit, but he possesses also the modern sense of brotherhood with all that lives. Distinction is one of his qualities. He seeks excellence in style, not singularity.

This is not a biography—Mr. Swartwout is anything but dead—rather is it a panegyric of modern American monumental architecture as represented by one of its most distinguished interpreters.

Much has been written on the theme that the characteristic of our time in architecture is chaos. The civilizations of the past have each had their distinctive style, but the present day is marked by the practice of imitating simultaneously all the ancient styles with more or less adaptation to present needs. This, by many, is looked upon as a sign of decadence, as an evil that must be fought. This noisy element must have novelty no matter what the cost. In the excess of their innovating zeal they clamor for "something different" and applaud every new movement, not because it is beautiful, or practical, or appropriate, but because it is new. To these iconoclasts all new forms are good and all old forms bad.

Mr. Swartwout has hurled mighty thunderbolts at these gentry in his writings. The vulgar and the meretricious arouse his ire and the eccentric and bizarre his contempt. But he has done more than just rail at these fools who no doubt think they are preparing the way for the angels. He has demonstrated in marble and stone that old forms can be made to clothe truth in the vesture of beauty and that for an architectural detail to be old is not for it to be dead, but rather, to be nearer immortality.

The Missouri State Capitol is not a thing of beauty simply because it is Roman in style but because it has line and proportion and harmony of the parts; because the bald structure is poetized with decorative forms that produce an esthetic emotion. The United States Post Office and Custom House at Denver is not a joy to the eye just because it is Greek in character but because it has common sense as a basis; because by its aspect and proportions it reveals thought and sentiment. In designing the George Washington Memorial, or the Macon Auditorium, Mr. Swartwout has not invented new forms and he has borrowed from the past in his design of his other monumental buildings, the Mary Baker Eddy Memorial, the Milford Memorial Hall and the Elks Memorial recently completed in Chicago. But in every one of his buildings there is personality and character. They are not mere replicas or adaptations. In each, there is originality, sameness with a difference, a rare splendor of imagination, a melody of utterance that make them stand out as monuments to good taste. He is never cryptic or eccentric, and his work is fastidiously unexaggerated and guarded against all violence. Because of this he has brought

distinction, if not glory, upon modern American
monumental architecture, or, if you prefer, on modern monumental architecture.

Against this evidence of the effectiveness of the
old art vocabulary in this age of jazz, what have the
apostles of novelty and nationalism to offer? "If
it has been the habit of painters in the past to represent the moon as silvery and round, merely because
it happens to look that way, the field of the earnest
modernist seeking for a new and wonderful expression is obviously limited to fancy and not to fact.
He must make a square moon, or a heart-shaped
one, or one of some other pleasing shape and he
must paint it pink or green if he wants to be modern."
The quotation is from Mr. Swartwout's writings
and the idea it voices applies to architecture as well
as to painting. We have seen quantities of square
moons on canvas already and we may yet see buildings built on the cubistic formula. Sanity may not
be imposed by statute.

It is heartening however, to find men like Mr.
Swartwout striking effective blows in defense of
rationalism and showing by actual example what
may be done with the old architectural alphabet.

if mortal man had the longevity of marble, one
might understand the impatience of an Athenian

gazing for two thousand years upon a Corinthian or Doric temple, but fortunately, or otherwise, we live but a few short years, not long enough for beauty to pall upon us. As a matter of fact we have more diversity than had the contemporaries of the Parthenon, or those of the Roman, Gothic or Renaissance edifices. Instead of being environed by buildings all of the same architectural "style" and being weighed down by a monotony of excellence, we have all that has survived to pick from, and whatever survives is good.

To take this "good" and adapt it to new sites, new needs, new uses, is to continue an esthetic tradition that has been upheld for centuries and which for that reason, if for no other, cannot be wrong. "All design," Mr. Swartwout has said, "is adaptation to a great extent; sometimes deliberate, sometimes unconscious. It is not copying; it is the occasional use of motifs the idea for which someone else has taken from the work of some previous designer. No architect has ever, with a vacant mind and a clean sheet of paper, evolved from his own inner consciousness a perfectly original building."

He has been inspired by the Greeks in his design of the Mary Baker Eddy Memorial, that is to say he has used the alphabet used by the Greeks when they have wished to express Peace, Love, Harmony. The question is not, "is this modern monument Greek?" but "does it express Harmony, Love and Peace?"

In his latest work, the Elks National Memorial Headquarters Building in Chicago, the adaptation is not so apparent and the influence is more Roman than Greek, but it is a classic building for all that and devoid of all eccentricity.

It is a finely proportioned building, circular in form, with wings at the sides and rear, with the central dome, sixty-seven feet in diameter, rising ninety-four feet in height, supported on a noble colonnade of twenty-four columns. It rises on a plot of ground on the Lake front and faces on Lincoln Park so that it is viewed in the proper perspective, at the end of reasonably long vistas.

A series of steps and terraces serve as a pedestal, so that there is enough recession and elevation for the edifice to be seen to advantage even at close range. The problem was to provide a memorial room of an area of four thousand feet and a set of smaller rooms for offices and reception rooms. The memorial hall is the pivotal edifice, two stories and a cupola, and rectangular wings one story high flank it on the sides and rear. These wings are subsidiary to the main rotunda but contribute greatly to the general harmony of the monument. Open courts within the angles formed by the rear and side wings have been planted with trees and shrubs in order to bring the Park treatment into the picture.

The building is of Indiana limestone hand-finished up to the base of the columns. The decorative feature of the exterior is the frieze, about five feet high and very completely filled with figures in high relief. This circles the edifice and is a sculptural glorification of the Elks brotherhood. The South side portrays the glories of Peace, with an expression of the four cardinal virtues of the Elks' ritual, Charity, Justice, Brotherly Love and Fidelity. On the North side are depicted the horrors of War. The sculpture is by Adolph A. Weinman and the results obtained are of the highest artistic value.

The building is of Guastavino masonry, which carries the exterior stone dome. The inner face of the Guastavino foundation carries the panelled plaster domical ceiling, an ornate assemblage of coffers separated by a frame work of sculptured bands painted in rich colors and touched discreetly with gold. The hall itself is of marble up to the caps of the main order, except for certain panels in which mural paintings are set. The basic marble is a warmly tinted, slightly veined, white marble, while the columns are of Pavonezza, Skyros, Cippolino and other colored marble. The windows of the reception rooms and of the hallways on the main floor are of painted glass, in soft subdued color and grisaille, with a pattern recalling the Italian Renaissance.

In addition to beauty of structure, beauty of line and curve, balance and harmony of masses and dimensions, the rotunda will have to recommend it a skillful use of color. A memorial constructed entirely of white marble would have been cold and sepulchral. The rich ceiling, the polychrome columns, the delicately tinted windows lend warmth to the interior without taking away any of its dignity.

The reception rooms in the back wing, while less pretentious in size and ornamentation, constitute an important item in the general scheme and the arrangement of them is felicitous in the extreme. They are disposed en enfilade, one large oval salon in the center, immediately back of the rotunda, and two smaller circular rooms opening from it, right and left. The two smaller reception rooms also open diagonally onto the great hall through wide vestibules so that one reception room may be used by itself or all three as a suite. These rooms are panelled to the ceiling, the Grand Reception Room in English Oak and the two smaller reception rooms in American Oak.

Mr. Swartwout showed his orginality by making a round building where precedent and specifications indicated a square edifice as the orthodox form. The programme prepared by Col. J. Hollis Wells for the competition was written around the Scottish Rite Hall in Washington. This edifice may be said to have become the accepted type for Fraternal buildings and most of the designs submitted in the competition were based upon a square rectangular construction. That Mr. Swartwout won the competition is the best proof that could be offered that architecture is not a matter of formulas.

It is all very well to teach undergraduates in the schools of architecture that the Corinthian column is twenty modules high, the entablature five, the base one, and the capital seventy minutes, but mastering this will not give them a sense of proportion. Mr. Swartwout has a greater number of positive ideas than any artist-writer that ever I have known and he possesses wonderful intrepidity and skill in expounding or defending them. Writing about formulas, he has said that "most standards are minimum standards" and that, "if we should ever start to apply pure logic to architecture, there would be little architecture left.''

The secret of all art is, first find your truth and then choose the best possible way of dressing it. In architecture, beauty and truth go hand in hand. A lie in architecture, a fictitious structure which hides the real idea instead of expressing it, is never beautiful. Mr. Swartwout knows the truth and knows how to dress it. What is more, he likes to tell it, which is contrary to the axiom that speech was given to us as a means of concealing our thoughts.

In his fiery impatience of privilege, authority and commercialism, in his recoil from the ugliness of modern realities, he has spoken out, in and out of meeting, and called things by their real names. When he has said, ''I have no tolerance for the mistaken groups of individuals who, being in temporary control of the policies of an institution, proclaim loudly their own policies as being the only correct policies of all right-thinking people,'' he has voiced the feelings of many a brow-beaten artist too poor, or too mercenary, to resist the ukase of Philistines. He has also said, ''I have no respect for these middlemen who call themselves architects and who by modern business methods acquire a large practice and build up a reputation upon the work and design of hired employees. In Wren's time commissions were given to an architect because he was a good artist and not because he was a good business man, or a good solicitor."

Although good business men and good solicitors will continue to secure commissions, it is well for a line to be drawn between them and those architects who are merely artists. Artists do count in the universal scheme, even if they do not elbow out of their way the materialists and the "go getters." A good building lives a long time and the perpetrator of a poor building will also find that a poor building remains to haunt him and expose his littleness. The evidence may not be hidden. It took two hundred and twenty years to build the temple of Diana at Ephesus, and twenty thousand artists and workmen were occupied twenty-two years in the construction of the mausoleum of Shagehan at Agra, but nowadays, the architect can in his lifetime build a dozen monuments and each will bear mute and eloquent testimony of his ability, and it will not be his ability as a business man that will show but his merit as an artist.

Let Mr. Swartwout then take heart.

J. SANFORD SALTUS

CYPRIEN BOULET, *Painter*
(PARIS, 1919)

J. SANFORD SALTUS

"A Soft, Meek, Patient, Humble, Tranquil Spirit Who Did Good by Stealth and Blushed to Find it Fame"

H E never spoke out. Upon these four words, gathered from a private letter, Matthew Arnold constructed a complete and intimate picture of the poet, Thomas Gray.

In writing of the late J. Sanford Saltus, whom it was my privilege and honor to count as friend and confidant, I cannot do better than to borrow Matthew Arnold's text, as it fits better than could any eulogistic epitaph the character of the man whose left hand gave so much without the least knowledge of it ever reaching his right.

Although Mr. Saltus was sixty-eight years old when in a moment of absentmindedness he drained a poisonous solution with which he was brightening some old coins, he was a man who had become old too young and whose life was spent in meditation and the slippered occupations that come with declining years and departed energy. So sensitive was he in private life, so modest in public, that the thoughts that arose in him never got full utterance. Widowed in 1906 from a wife with whom he had enjoyed twenty years of perfect mutual understanding, a woman of rare talent as a painter, whose conception of the beautiful coincided in nearly every point with his own almost childish admiration for noble visions and noble deeds, he lived in semi-seclusion in a quiet family hotel on Madison Avenue and in travel abroad, principally in France.

I met him more than twenty years ago at the Salmagundi Club and I knew him then as an amateur painter of uneven talent and the good angel of the Club of which he was one of the founders. His dress, his manner, his mode of living, gave no intimation whatever of the fact that he had inherited a large furtune from his father, the late Theodore Saltus, a steel manufacturer who made the first cannon to be fashioned in this country from American steel.

He had a diffident way with him, a certain bashful, embarrassed timidity, that until you got to know him intimately made him appear as lacking in social instinct and provincial in his thoughts.

Burke, in one of his speeches, made use of a simile that will be apposite at this point. Said the great orator and statesman, "Because half a dozen grasshoppers under a fern make the field ring with their importunate chink, whilst thousands of great cattle, reposed beneath the shadow of ancient oaks, chew the cud and are silent, do not imagine that those who make the noise are the only inhabitants of the field."

J. Sanford Saltus, like Thomas Gray, "never spoke out," but although inarticulate, he had under this reticence a soul attuned to beauty and a heart that was pure gold. Many human grasshoppers are listed in Who's Who, and some have statues erected to their memory on the highways. The staid and humble subject of this biography is not listed in any directory of our great, or near-great, contemporaries but if great deeds lift little men to their level, his title to greatness is clearer than those of most of the press-agented notables of our day.

Because of a delicate constitution he was educated at home, under the supervision of private tutors, and this perhaps served to develop in him that shyness which children generally shed by constant contact with their fellows in school.

The principle of dog eat dog, prevalent in most of our present-day business, being abhorrent to him, he took up the study of painting and studied here for a time at the Art Students' League and under Carroll Beckwith, J. Francis Murphy, and Frank E. Scott. He was also for a time a pupil at the École des Beaux Arts in Paris, but being exceedingly modest in his own appreciation of his talent as an artist, he always disclaimed credit as an executant and preferred to enroll himself as a spectator and a generous applauder of the good work of others.

In 1908 he founded the John Sanford Saltus prize to be awarded yearly by the National Academy of Design for a painting or piece of sculpture by any artist, man or woman, American or foreign. He followed this up in 1910 by giving to the École des Beaux Arts in Paris an endowment sufficient for the yearly award of a prize of 500 francs to the author of the best war picture exhibited during the year. He is also the donor of an annual gold medal which is awarded by the Art Students' League, and many are the art students in Paris whom he helped in an unobtrusive manner.

Although I had known him for many years it was not until I heard that he had given the greater part of the $35,000 used in erecting the equestrian statue of Joan of Arc at 93rd Street and Riverside Drive that I realized that my frugal and unassuming friend was a rich man. He had from time to time contributed modest sums to various war charities organized by me for the relief of the families of French artists serving at the front, and as I sat with him as a member of the Board of Trustees of the Museum of French Art, I knew of his great admiration for

French art and of his great love for the French people. He had received the decoration of Officer of Public Instruction and of Chevalier du Mérite Agricole from France and after his donation of the Joan of Arc statue was made a Knight and then an Officer of the Legion of Honor, but he bore his honors meekly and promptly turned the conversation aside whenever an attempt was made to draw from him an account of what he had done to merit these honors.

I, personally, knew of his having given a Joan of Arc statue to the Church of the Port at Nice and of his having contributed liberally to the fund for the erection of the statues of King Edward the Seventh at Cannes and of Queen Victoria at Nice, but it was not until after his death that I heard he had also given statues of Joan of Arc to the cities of Blois, Rouen and the town of Domrémy in France, to the Cathedral of St. John the Divine in New York, the Winchester Cathedral in England and the City of New Orleans.

A man of deep religious feeling, he had been thrilled by the zeal and patriotism of the Lily Maid of France and had enlisted under her banner. He had also at one time evinced a sentimental interest in Louis XVII, the young son of the unfortunate Louis XVI, whose tragic fate during the turbulent days of the French revolution easily awakened his sympathies, and he had collected a large library of books which he subsequently donated to the Salmagundi Club, in which the history, real or supposed, of the Dauphin is treated from every angle.

Another one of his enthusiasms was the collection of medals and ancient coins, a passion which may have caused his death, since it is by drinking a fluid with which he was cleaning some of these medals that he came to his untimely end. Not only was he a member of the council of the American Numismatic Society but he had the distinction of being the Vice-President of the British Numismatic Society and President of the Numismatic Club of this city.

He was a collector, however, who collected for others. He assembled what is probably the largest and most complete collection of medals struck off in honor of Joan of Arc during the past two hundred years, but as soon as he had gathered it together he promptly turned it over to the Numismatic Society, already the recipient from him of a complete collection of foreign orders.

He made the same gesture when he purchased Henry Chartier's painting "Hurrah for the Nation," a brilliant piece of charging cavalry, which had won the Saltus prize for 1912. This spirited battle painting he donated to the Museum of French Art, just as he had donated his books to the Salmagundi

Club and his medals to the Numismatic Society.

When I conceived the plan of decorating the Library of New York University with busts of famous American artists, one of the men I turned to, to help finance the project, was naturally enough J. Sanford Saltus. There was an apparent slackening of interest on the part of the friends of the late Carroll Beckwith and it looked as if I would have difficulty in collecting the full amount needed to pay for the cost of the memorial. In a casual letter written to Mr. Saltus, then in Nice, I mentioned the slow progress I was making but never hinting in any way that I expected him to come to the rescue. As a matter of fact he had already made a very liberal donation towards the cost of erecting the memorial and I felt sure that the deficiency would eventually be made up through contributions from former pupils of the painter, a number of whom had remained deaf to the first appeal.

In just exactly the number of days required for my letter to travel from New York to Nice, I received the visit of an employe of Mr. Saltus' bankers who announced to me that upon cable advice received from Mr. Saltus they had pleasure in handing me a check for the full amount of the deficiency. Mr. Saltus himself never wrote me about it and ignored the incident completely when I referred to it in subsequent correspondence.

I also interested him in the memorial to Cardinal Mercier, also at New York University, and in the fund for reconstructing the Library of the University of Louvain. I had discussed with him the founding of a chair of Art at New York University and he had authorized me to offer $75,000. to the university towards that end when death put an end to my negotiations with Chancellor Brown of the university. His chief concern at the time was to share the credit for this endowment or foundation with others. He wished others to contribute to a general fund which would not bear his name.

Still consumed with that spirit of unselfish giving he was quick to take up my suggestion of a bust to Poe and commissioned me to negotiate with Daniel Chester French for the memorial which now adorns the Hall of Fame of New York University. Together we had planned a room for the Louvain Library in which an effigy of Joan of Arc would ornament a monumental chimney and he had made a preliminary donation towards it.

His donations are only known incompletely. One of his most important gifts was the Foundation which bears his name and which he created for the benefit of the French Museum. This was a bequest of over $100,000. the income of which is used to bring lecturers on French Art to America. He gave a yearly silver cup to the Fencers Club, of which he was at one time Vice-President, and time and again came to the aid of the French Y. M. C. A. of this City when that organization was in financial difficulties. The hospitals and relief organizations of Nice, where he spent many winters, have lost in him a generous patron. He was a frequent visitor to England and the statue of Shakespeare in Southwark Cathedral in London is one of his donations.

Between times he wrote books which in his modesty he caused to be privately printed. He is the author of several monographs on Louis XVII, of a book on "the flowers and animals that Shakespeare loved," of a volume of "Impressions of the Oberammergau Passion Play" and of a book on "the Statues of New York," published by Putnam's in 1923, a few weeks after his death.

This last is a descriptive catalogue of the statues erected within the city limits as memorials to individuals. He was looking forward to the appearance of this book as filling a void. In his feeling of civic pride he wanted to circulate more widely a knowledge of the sculpture ornamenting our public places.

He had planned to present busts of Benjamin West, Peale and Gilbert Stuart to complete the series in the Library of New York University and nothing was further from his mind than the thought of death. I saw him last in Paris, less than six weeks before his death, and our talk was all of plans for the future. He had everything to live for and no suspicion that he made away with himself must be allowed to darken his memory. A charming woman whom he had known from his early manhood and who had been his lifelong friend had consented to marry him and the ceremony was to have taken place in Paris during the coming winter.

In addition to the activities which I have indicated, Mr. Saltus was a Fellow of the National Academy of Design; a patron of the American Museum of Natural History; a Life Member and Honorary Vice-President of the Museum of French Art, French Institute in the United States; Life Member of the Metropolitan Museum of Art; honorary member of the Art Students' League; Fencers Club; Salmagundi Club; Archæological Institute of America; and member of the Gypsy Lore Society of England.

He was blessed with credulity, "that soothing hand that strokes keen thought to slumber." "He never spoke out," but he furnished inspiration to many and his memory will endure.

SAINT GAUDENS

John Flanagan, *Sculptor*

SAINT GAUDENS

IF there is any virtue in the saying "Home is where the heart is," he that was America's greatest sculptor is now happy in having reached home. His body may lie among the rugged hills of Vermont, but his spirit is here, in this Hall of Remembrance, where soon his Diana will tower and shimmer in the sunlight of University Heights, and where all about him are the effigies and memories of those he loved best in life.

This very building in which his bust will be enshrined is the creation of two of his near-brothers, his pals of early manhood, I refer to Stanford White and Charles F. McKim. Keeping him silent company in this rotunda are others whom he called "friend." Here is J. Q. A. Ward. Here is William M. Chase. Here is Carroll Beckwith, and here is Walter Shirlaw. Each of these men came close to Saint Gaudens and loved him, as he them, and he is at home in their company.

I wish to thank Mr. Blashfield and the members of the National Academy of Design for making the dedication of these busts a part of the centennial celebration of the National Academy. The gesture is particularly fine since in his youth Saint Gaudens headed a rebellion against the Academy. This, however, was only a lover's quarrel, and at the height of his fame Saint Gaudens found himself again in sympathy with academic standards. Indeed, Saint Gaudens considered himself a product of the Academy. When a mere boy he followed its evening courses. Here, in the old Italian Doge's palace on 23rd Street, after a laborious day spent at the lathe of a cameo cutter, he worked from 8 to 11 P. M., transferring to paper the plaster casts of Greek and Roman statuary of the Academy. Although his first modeling lessons were those he obtained in France at the École des Beaux Arts, it was at the Academy that he schooled his eye and his hand in the preliminary art of drawing.

Others will tell you of the remarkable career of this giant, whom White disrespectfully called "Dear old Hoss" and "My beloved Snooks." I will only touch on a paragraph of his reminiscences, where he writes that upon reading Plutarch's Lives, he made the great resolve "to be the most lovable man that ever was."

This resolve Saint Gaudens kept, and there are many here today who were made the beneficiaries of this love. He was beloved of Whistler, whose spe-

cialty was making enemies, and such aloof person-
ages as Rodin and Robert Louis Stevenson found
pleasure in his society, and felt deep affection for
him.

His heart was attuned to beauty and it opened as
wide for Paris and for Rome as it did for Dublin,
where he was born, or for New York, where his
boyhood and seventeen of his adult years were spent.
Many who are here remember his studios in the
Sherwood, at 57th Street and Sixth Avenue, and at
148 West 36th Street. I only met him once, in Paris
in 1900, at the time of the Exposition, where he
was a member of the jury on sculpture and I was a
Commissioner in charge of the decorative end of the
American exhibits. He was supervising the installa-
tion of his magnificent Sherman group, and I remember how childishly pleased he was at the ava-
lanche of compliments that fell upon him from the
lips of all then present. He loved Paris and the
French. It is not strange, considering that all his
paternal forbears came from the rugged hill country
on the French side of the Pyrenees.

It was in Paris that he created his masterpieces,
the Farragut monument and the equestrian group of
Sherman escorted by Victory. He appreciated the
training which he had received at the École des

Beaux Arts, and when he spoke or wrote of the proposed American Academy of Fine Arts in Rome, which he subsequently helped to bring about, he wished it to be modeled on the French institution which is a post-graduate adjunct of the École, I mean the Villa Medici, where the winners of the Prix de Rome devote four years to study under earnest, classical guidance. In a speech which he delivered in Washington, at a time when funds were being raised for the endowment of the American Academy of Fine Arts in Rome, he voiced the conviction that the "result of the serious education required by the system of the École des Beaux Arts was that those who did not attain to high achievement at least became better workmen in the vocation they eventually entered." He did not believe in superficial knowledge, nor in gaining ends in the quickest possible way. He was a conscientious worker, and the fact that he spent eighteen years on the Shaw monument and ten years on the Sherman group is eloquent testimony to the fact that with him nothing was good enough until it was perfect.

Because of this respect for training, this appreciation that art must be taught, I venture to speak to you today of a project which I know would have been dear to the heart of Saint Gaudens, and which might now be brought to consummation as his legacy to American artists to come.

In the course of my recent visit to the Exposition of Modern Decorative Art in Paris, I was brought in contact with the French Minister of Fine Arts and the directors of the École des Beaux Arts, and secured from them the assurance that if the United States raised an endowment similar to that which now insures the operation and maintenance of the American Academy in Rome, the French government and the École des Beaux Arts would create a series of Prix de Paris similar in character to the existing Prix de Rome, and facilitate for American students of architecture and the fine arts the acquiring of an art education in Paris as complete as that given in Rome.

The École des Beaux Arts would concede free tuition to the American winners of these Prix de Paris, and procure their admission into the ateliers of the best French painters and sculptors. The endowment would only be needed for the housing and maintenance of the winners of these scholarships, and every American university maintaining a department of architecture or a chair of fine arts would be invited to enter candidates for these scholarships.

I have sounded the opinion of a great many of the

heads of these universities, and the prospect of a four year post-graduate course in Paris is proving alluring to the majority of them. Many of you have studied in Paris, and all who have, retain, I am sure, a deep sense of the benefits to be acquired from this study. Modest as are the wants of an art student, there are yet certain needs of a material character which, if they are difficult to obtain, operate as a damper of enthusiasm and chiller of artistic inspiration. In olden days kings and princes fostered the arts by guaranteeing the artists against material worries. A Saint Gaudens foundation providing for the free tuition of a score or more of American art students in Paris would be a hot-house where the flowering of American artistic genius would be effected with certainty and ease.

Those who knew Saint Gaudens will agree with me that no one ever approved and obliged with a nobler and more unreserving promptitude of soul. I believe that this characteristic is not rare among artists, but, unfortunately, as a class they are poor in money, however rich they may be in spiritual wealth. Each of you, however, knows a rich man, and each of you may assist his entry into the kingdom of art by winning him over as a contributor to some fund such as I have outlined for the creation of a Saint Gaudens foundation.

Recently, Professor Dewey of Columbia bemoaned the fact that "disinterested love of inquiry and idealistic devotion to the things of the mind in science and art are not flourishing in our universities as are the studies that prepare for what is called practical life." The members of the National Academy of Design here present will rejoice, I am sure, at the spectacle of this university erecting altars to painters and sculptors and providing classes and lectures for the awakening and developing of an art conscience among its students.

The history of American art does not recede very far into the past, but one of its earliest chapters mentions the fact that New York University took the pioneer step of establishing a professorship of the Literature of the Art of Design ninety years ago. The first incumbent of this chair was Samuel F. B. Morse, founder and president of the National Academy, and some day I cherish the hope of your placing the bust of the Academy's founder in this Hall of Remembrance.*

The university has recently realized an ambition which I and a great many of you had long fostered, in that it has obtained, through Colonel Friedsam, the financial support of the Altman Foundation for its art department. I foresee the time when addi-

*This was realized in May, 1928

tional donations from other art lovers will permit the university to construct a special building devoted not only to the teaching of the history of art, but to its technique. On that day we may see these busts removed from this Rotunda and installed in the university's museum. We shall soon have Whistler here, and after him Sargent, and later—much later I hope—the busts of many who are here today doing reverence to the memory of a great artist, in whose footsteps they walk sure-footed and unafraid.

Many are the statues that have outlived the fame of those that wrought them. Frederick the Great still lives but Rauch is forgotten. Who remembers Sergell or Quarnstrom, or Wyatt, or Gibson, and how faded is the fame of Canova and Thorwaldsen. No such fate is reserved for Saint Gaudens, and our grandsons will not look upon the memorials of Shaw, Farragut or Sherman as the work of an anonymous sculptor.

His was no trivial greatness. His fame is secure.

CLINTON OGILVIE
Paul W. Bartlett, *Sculptor*

CLINTON OGILVIE

In one of his lectures on "Considerations on Painting," John La Farge lays down as an axiom that a painting "gives most indubitable testimony of the moral state of its painter." A work of art is ever an expression of the man who wrought it. Individuality exists among artists, and originality, but all artists of the same nationality, painting during the same period, show characteristics that identify the painter as belonging to a certain race and to a certain time.

There are periods in the world history when art seems to be obscured, when beauty is eclipsed by famine or wars or ignorance, or banished from the earth by bigotry or utilitarian demands more insistent than the hunger of the soul for narcissi. Between the Greek and Roman flowering of the arts and their rebirth at the time of the Renaissance there occurred five centuries of darkness in which it seemed that even the memory of beauty had been lost.

Here, in our time, after a colonial period in which the arts were in favor, and polished manners among the aristocracy the rule, there came a dismal era of drab utilitarianism, when the crayon enlargement over the horse-hair sofa flourished and cast-iron stags became statuary.

In this age of ugliness, Clinton Ogilvie was born. A descendant of the proud house of Airlie, renowned through Scotch history, "for their loyaltie to their Prince," he grew up amid prosaic surroundings, the son of well-to-do parents but the inheritor of Spartan virtues and ascetic tendencies. There was nothing to particularly incline him to the study of art in his disposition, save, perhaps, a natural awe for certain manifestations of nature that gave rise for a time to apprehension lest he develop into a man of moody silence and morose introspection. Like his distinguished ancestor, Sir Alexander Ogilvy, immortalized in the famous ballad of the battle of Harlaw as:

> "The gracious gude Lord Ogilvy
> Renownit for truth and equity
> For faith and magnanimity,"

he was a devout Christian, shrinking from anything violent, or brusque, or bizarre and with a mind and soul that were the sanctuary of ideas of *noblesse* and *droiture*.

A friend of the painter James M. Hart, born in Scotland, but in after life a landscape painter of note in America, young Ogilvie was first initiated into the mysteries of painting in Hart's studio. After a season in Dusseldorf, where Hart studied under Schirmer, Hart in 1856 had opened a studio in New York. Young Ogilvie, then eighteen years old, absorbed the *manière* of Hart, and being anything but a revolutionist, copied his master and repeated his errors. He had less knowledge than Hart, but more enthusiasm, less reflection and thought, less ponderation, but more spontaneity, less science, less *métier*, but a certain feeling, a certain harmony, and he soon set out on his own.

Nourished on tradition, orthodox as to technique and holding fast to what was good in the art expression of the day, he affirmed his personality through the influence of John F. Kensett whose studio he frequented for a while. In some of his early pictures, the dense growth of trees on a rocky ledge, the weeds, vines, gnarled trunks overgrown with moss, and all the debris of the primeval forest, are rendered with the same literal minuteness that characterizes the work of Kensett.

When but twenty-six years old he was elected an Associate of the National Academy of Design.

It was at one of the exhibitions of the Academy that he met the gentle and talented woman whom

he shortly thereafter selected, with most excep-
tional felicity, to be his wife. This romance, which
continued unclouded to the last day of his life,
changed him from a shy and withdrawn poet, much
given to long and solitary contemplation of nature,
to a genial, tolerant philosopher with a lively sense
of brotherhood with life and all of God's creatures.

Helen Slade, descended from one of the most aris-
tocratic New England families, with a British ancestry that included a knight of the ancient Order of
the Garter, herself an amateur painter of great prom-
ise, was drawn towards the fastidiously honest
young artist by their mutual horror of the commonplace, their jealous worship of beauty, their quick
response to knightly sentiments. She convinced the
inarticulate and diffident youth entering apologet-
ically upon an artistic career that all his geese were
swans and that he could discard the corks of method
and tradition that were helping him to float and
swim out for himself unaided.

They were married in the bride's home on Mur-
ray Hill, an imposing mansion off Fifth Avenue
with a garden running through from 38th to 39th
Street. The wedding was a social event that brought
together the first families of nascent New York society. The young couple had good looks, health,

youth, talent, social position and high character in common and never was there a marital union entered into with greater guarantees of lasting happiness. The honeymoon was spent in Europe, mostly in France, and some of the best landscapes painted by Clinton Ogilvie date from that period.

At no time is there in his work excess of innovating zeal, he was ever a conservative, but his canvases are less austere, his subjects more sprightly than the earlier product of his brush.

The treatment of landscape in England and the Colonies previous to Constable, involved a rich brown tone, with the accompaniment of coloring which was purely a matter of convention. Constable insisted that the earth and trees were green and not brown. The early American landscape painters, Durand, Cole and Doughty, saw and painted in accordance with the tenets of Constable, but Ogilvie's first principles were acquired through the too faithful imitation of Hart and Kensett, whose tone was brown rather than green. Ogilvie had occasion at this time to study at first hand the work of that interesting group of French painters who have since become famous as the Barbizon group. Canvases of this period by Rousseau, Corot, Millet, Diaz, Troyon, Daubigny and Dupré show nature in a gladsome mood, with the sun shining and the atmosphere clear.

George Inness, visiting France at the moment of the flowering of this school of outdoor painting, abandoned his early manner, which had been purely objective and full of intricate elaborate detail, to adopt the more subjective manner of Rousseau. But a Scotch ancestry running back many centuries to Gilchrist, Earl of Angus, makes one respectful of tradition. A recent writer has observed that "the accompaniments of the Reformation have lain a blight on Scottish arts and affairs." Robert Burns to the contrary notwithstanding, the Scotch as a race are more literal than poetical. Ogilvie possessed all the defects and all the qualities characteristic of the sons of "the bonnie house of Airlie." Where the French rushed in, the Scot feared to tread. He saw the painters of the Fontainebleau region riding roughshod over every routine regulation, disregarding all the sacred canons of Academic art and wrestling only with what they saw, but he was afraid to follow them. La Farge's axiom that a painting gives indubitable testimony of the character, or the "moral state," of the painter, is supported by the canvases left by Ogilvie. They grow less sombre, more joyful as he matures, but they are always scrupulously drawn, meticulously "finished," elaborately detailed.

Inness, Alexander Wyant, Homer D. Martin, Ralph Blakelock modified their way of painting and the character of their composition after they had mastered the principles of the Barbizon painters, but Ogilvie adhered to the "honest way" of painting and did not overcome difficulties of drawing by "happy" arrangement of color masses. Marvellous in accurate imitation are the various objects in the foreground of his pictures: the golden-rod seems to wave, the blackberry to glisten; leaves, grasses, weeds, stones are so carefully finished that we seem not to be looking at a distant prospect but lying on the ground with herbage and blossom directly under our eyes.

His best works, "Path by the River," "Farmington River," "In the Woods," "Afternoon on the Avon," "The White Birch," "The Brook," "Near Jackson in the White Mountains," show evidence of deep thought and well garnered knowledge: knowledge of the laws of painting as of the laws of nature; knowledge of light and air, of sunshine and shadow, of mountain, of forest, of gleaming waterfall and placid lake, of every tree found within the leafy haunts of our great forests, from the graceful birch to the sombre pine and the melancholy cypress.

To those who like a veil over their landscapes, his painting may be too explicative, too literal, yet in spite of its explicitness, it evokes deep emotion and what greater test of real art can there be than the stirring of the heart through the eyes. He likes to paint the tender moment of the day, when the countryside lies in dreamful languishment. One gets visions of delectable hills, cool-shadowed valleys, green fields stretching far away to the misty horizon, great cloud islands moving slowly in an atmosphere of purple peacefulness. He likes the healing silence of the forest with its old shaggy hemlocks and its carpet of glossy, dry, dead beech leaves. One feels the benedictive calm of his woodland scenes, they are benignly fragrant, restful unspeakably.

The painting of landscape is subject to perhaps the greatest abuse of any department of art. There is perhaps no other in which the hand of incompetency so boldly displays itself. To paint the figure requires a serious knowledge of form and anatomy and a cognizance of the most exquisite niceties of color, light and shade. The same rule applies to the painting of cattle, and all forms of still life demand accuracy of observation, skill of draftsmanship and a mastery of the rendition of colors and textures. In landscape, the tyro who can neither draw nor paint, but who has been schooled in a few tricks of brush and palette, produces what passes for an effect and is supposed to constitute a picture.

The true landscape painter however, remains as great an artist as the painter of history. To him, nature is as living a thing as humanity itself. In landscape painting there is a greater variety of objects, textures and phenomena to reproduce. Nor is it devoid of expression. It may be void of passion, but it never is of sentiment. A landscape can be tranquil or spirit-stirring. Its seasons—sunrise, sunset, the storm, the calm; various kinds of trees, herbage, waters, mountains, skies—whatever scene is chosen, a mood pervades the whole. Light and darkness tremble in the atmosphere and it is not too much to affirm that had the talent of Raphael been applied to landscape his productions would have been as great as those he produced in his chosen field.

Painting is a means of expression, as is music and poetry. The painter reaches forth for his ideal according to his intellectual bent, his spiritual temperament, and whether he paints his poem in the Homeric or the Virgilian mood depends upon his "moral state," his surroundings, the age in which he paints, the "style" of the hour and the racial

characteristics inherited from a long line of ances-
tors. Those who like to speculate upon the relative
power of environment and heredity may reflect upon
the fact that Ogilvie was in France at the time when
Claude Monet was battling against a public opinion
which found his brilliant canvases too unorthodox
for the day and hour. He was not the one to dispar-
age the artistic effectiveness of Monet and of his fol-
lowers in the newly created school of impressionism,
but it is to be noted that he continued faithful to his
Gods and was uninfluenced by the clamor raised all
about him over the rising of this radical constella-
tion in the serene firmament of art.

His views of Killarney, of Brunsmoor in Switzer-
land, of the hill of the Madonna in Mentone, the
nature studies painted in Cannes, Vichy, Auteuil,
Monacco, Arjéles, Hyéres, are perhaps more brilliant in coloring than his landscapes of the Adiron-
dacks and the White Mountains but this is because
the sunlight is more violent on the Riviera than
along the Hudson and not because the painter has
yielded to the influence of the painters around him,
all more or less intent on creating a shining tumult
of many colors. Never invoking the assistance of a
great or sensational subject, but sedulously seeking
for the simplest material, Clinton Ogilvie has by his

skill and feeling taught us the beauty and poetry of subjects that have been called meagre and void of interest. By painting conscientiously he has remained "loyal to his Prince" like a true son of the house of Airlie.

The pictures of the great Italian masters have stood best the criticism of ages. They are produced on principles of truth and not on any abstract notion of the sublime or the beautiful. These artists were gifted with a keen perception of the beauty in nature and they imitated nature in simplicity and with single-heartedness. They were honest and without affectation, they had no theories and painted what they saw.

Ogilvie was true to "the God of things as they are." His paintings hang in the Metropolitan Museum of Art and the National Gallery in Washington. The Hall of Remembrance of American Artists in New York University contains his bust alongside of those of Saint Gaudens, Inness and Chase, J. Q. A. Ward and Henry Kirke Brown, Whistler and Duveneck. He had placed his faith in "unerring Nature, at once the source and end and test of art," and he possessed "nameless graces which no methods teach." He died on November 28, 1900, after sixty-two years of devotion to duty and to the loftiest ideals, and his disconsolate widow has placed memorials to him in the Cathedral of Saint John the Divine, the National Academy of Design, the Metropolitan Museum of Art, and the National Gallery at Washington.

He was "gracious and gude" like his forebear of 1411, a lover of Truth and Equity and "renownit," not only for "Faith and Magnanimity," but for a hand and soul that could paint the splendor of Nature,

> "When pensive twilight comes slowly on
> To meet the evening star."

SAMUEL F. B. MORSE

HORATIO GREENOUGH (1841), *Sculptor*

SAMUEL F. B. MORSE

W E are met here today to do honor to a distinguished American who has added to the fame of this nation in what was once considered a field beyond cultivation—or at least left uncultivated because it was unremunerative—by a race of men supposedly given over to the pursuit of the "Almighty Dollar."

While it is true that Mexico and Lima had academies of art long before New York or Philadelphia, and while no public gallery of art existed in the City of New York until 1867, the reproach that ours is a material country may be refuted easily by pointing out the achievements in the fine arts of a group of Americans who worshipped beauty and strove valiantly to reproduce it at a time when the United States as a nation was only a few days old.

West and Copley, while they prospered and achieved their fame in England, were natives of Pennsylvania and Massachusetts, and John Trumbull, Gilbert Stuart, Edward G. Malbone, Washington Allston, Thomas Sully, Charles R. Leslie, C. Wilson Peale, Robert Fulton, practiced their art in these benighted States, where all had, more or less, to paint pot-boilers at from $5 to $50 each in order to live. In 1771, John Hancock paid Copley the munificent sum of eight guineas, or $56, for his portrait.

The pursuit of art for art's sake is thus shown to have existed in this allegedly materialistic land from the day of its birth, and American artists of a hundred years ago should be reverenced the more for the hardships they had to endure and the lack of encouragement they received then.

West and Copley had early emigrated to London, West in 1763 and Copley in 1778, and thither in time went most of our artists of that period, if not to stay, at least to study. West, who had succeeded Sir Joshua Reynolds as President of the Royal Academy, opened his atelier to them, and at some time or other numbered among his pupils Trumbull, the two Peales, Malbone, Dunlap, Allston, Sully, Leslie, Fulton, and last, but not least, the artist whom we honor this day, Samuel F. B. Morse.

Upon the death of Morse in 1872, ceremonies were held at the National Capital, where the leading men of the nation assembled in the Hall of the House of Representatives and paid tribute to his memory. Speaker Blaine occupied the chair, having on his right hand Vice-President Colfax, while in the front row of seats facing the Speaker's desk, were President Grant and his cabinet, and members of the Supreme Court of the United States. Numerous speeches were delivered on this occasion and eulogistic messages were received from a score of cities of the United States and from a dozen foreign capitals. All these appreciations were published by order of Congress. Almost all of them extolled Morse as a scientist and ignored him as an artist.

Morse, like his contemporary, Robert Fulton, abandoned art for science because of the lack of encouragement found in this country during the formative period of our Republic. Who knows to what heights they might have attained in the field which had been their first choice, had they received here the same sort of patronage which Copley and West received in England.

Although Morse invented the telegraph in 1832, it was not until 1839 that he abandoned painting to devote himself to his invention. That his first love was art is attested in a letter written by him from New York University, under date of March 15, 1838, in which he stated his wish, "As soon as practicable to relieve myself of the cares of the telegraph, that I may have my time to devote, more strenuously than ever, to the execution of my picture and the benefit of the Academy and of the Arts."

Samuel Finley Breese Morse was born at Charlestown, Massachusetts, on the 27th day of April, 1791. He was the son of the Reverend Doctor Jedediah Morse, an eminent Congregational clergyman, well known as a writer of American geography. His maternal great-grandfather was the Reverend Doctor Samuel Finley, a former President of Princeton College. Upon graduating at Yale, in 1810, he enrolled as a pupil under Washington Allston, and when the latter returned to London, in August, 1811, Morse accompanied him and was placed by him under the aegis of Benjamin West, whose studio was ever open, and whose advice was ever available to the young men of his native land.

So well did Morse profit from the lessons of the master, that two years after his arrival in England he won the gold medal of the Adelphi Society of Arts for his "Dying Hercules" a figure modelled in clay from which he later painted a picture. His funds running low, however, he was compelled to return to the United States in the following year, and was unable to enter a more pretentious painting, the "Judgment of Jupiter," for the prize of fifty guineas offered by the Royal Academy. West, then President of the Royal Academy, wrote to Morse that had the picture remained for the exhibition, it would certainly have won the prize.

Returning to Boston in 1815, flushed with his success in England and ambitious to make a name for himself in his native town, the young artist found that no demand existed whatever for historical painting, and as the only return his art could bring him was in the field of portraiture he bravely engaged in this branch of it, gladly accepting fifteen dollars each for likenesses painted by him in Boston and New Hampshire. Removing to Charleston, South Carolina, at the invitation of Doctor Finley, his uncle, he was able to demand a higher price for his portraits, and we hear of him painting four portraits a week at the then respectable price of sixty dollars each.

After painting one hundred and fifty of these portraits, he had set aside a sufficient sum to permit him to return to historical painting, and it was at this time that he painted the picture of the House of Representatives in session, which is now on view in the Corcoran Gallery in Washington. He spent eighteen months making this painting, which is a large canvas, eight feet by nine, and being unable to sell it, sought a revenue from it by placing it on view for an admission fee of twenty-five cents. The painting was exhibited at a loss of several hundred dollars, and Morse removed to New York in 1822, once more doomed to painting portraits.

His fame in this branch of the art soon spread, however, and when the Corporation of New York decided to have a portrait of General LaFayette painted for the New York City Hall, it was Morse who received the commission. For this he received $700, a price which at once stamped him as "having arrived."

When Morse settled in New York in 1825, the fine arts were under the protection of an organization incorporated in 1808 by Robert R. Livingston, DeWitt Clinton and a group of prominent citizens and known as the American Academy of the Arts. Colonel Trumbull, the celebrated painter, was the President, but of the seven directors only one was an artist.

This directorate of non-artists was opposed to the opening of an art school in connection with the Academy, but during the summer the Academy's collection of antique casts was open to students in the mornings from six to eight o'clock. Frequently, however, the curator of the Academy neglected to open its doors and the students wishing to instruct themselves had to turn away disappointed.

The injured artists met in Morse's rooms and it was suggested that an association of artists be formed by those present "for the promotion of the

arts and the assistance of students." A second meeting was held on November 8, 1825, this time in the
rooms of the Historical Society, and at this meeting
the artists organized themselves into the New York
Drawing Association, with Morse as President. The
members met in the evenings, three times a week,
each member furnishing his own drawing materials;
the expense of light and fuel was shared by all
through equal contributions.

The American Academy of Arts made an attempt
to swallow the Drawing Association on the slim
pretext that its members were drawing from casts
loaned by the American Academy, but the artists
refused to be absorbed and returned the casts to the
Academy. Word was conveyed to the directors of
the Academy, however, that the artists were not
maintaining an attitude of antagonism and that
they would re-enter the fold of the Academy if the
direction of the Academy could be placed in the
hands of artists instead of in the hands of laymen,
as was then the case. After a period of negotiations,
it was agreed that the Academy would elect six
artists as directors, thereby placing the management of affairs in the hands of artists. The Associated Artists thereupon nominated six of their
number to the directorate.

When the election took place, however, it was found that only two of the six candidates chosen by the artists were elected. Resentful over this breach of faith, the two elected immediately resigned and the artists now resolved to organize a new Academy.

A meeting was called on January 14, 1826, and Morse presented a plan for an institution "which shall be truly liberal, which shall be mutually beneficial, and which shall really encourage the arts." Each member of the New York Drawing Association was asked to select fifteen professional artists, and the fifteen receiving the highest number of votes were authorized to elect not less than ten, or more than fifteen, other professional artists, residents in the city of New York, the whole body thus chosen to be called the "National Academy of the Arts of Design." Those remaining in the Association after such election who wished to belong to the new institution were declared students.

A few days later, on the 18th of January, 1826, the National Academy of Design was formally organized, with S. F. B. Morse as President and John L. Morton as Secretary.

In the American Academy, the formation of the new art institution was severely felt and harsh recriminations were voiced by its directors. The American Academy made strenuous efforts to counteract the progress of the infant National, but public sentiment was with the artists and the National grew as the American wilted.

The first exhibition of the National Academy of Design was opened on the 13th of May, 1826, in a room in the second story of a house on the southwest corner of Broadway and Reade Street, an ordinary dwelling not covering an area of more than twenty-five by fifty feet. It consisted of one hundred and seventy exhibits and was the first solely artistic effort at exhibition ever held in the United States.

On May 3, 1827, Morse, as President of the Academy, delivered an address to the students, on the occasion of the Academy's first anniversary, in the Chapel of Columbia College, then on Church Street opposite Park Place. In this address Morse reviewed the experiences of the National Academies of Art in the various countries of Europe, and more particularly the history of the Royal Academy of Arts of Great Britain, which had served as the model for the organization of the American institution. After pointing out that it was not until after the reign of George III that the arts of design had awakened in earnest from their long sleep in England, Morse reviewed the establishment in 1768 of the Royal Academy of Arts, with Sir Joshua Reynolds as first President. He stressed the point that "every profession in society knows best what measures are necessary for its own improvement," and that those National Academies were successful whose destinies were guided by artists, and not by laymen and so-called art patrons. He showed that in its first year of existence the Academy had been enabled to give free instruction to about thirty students. In urging harmony and the cooperation of all members, he laid particular emphasis upon the truth that "individual prosperity depends on the prosperity of the whole body." "The history of the arts in Britain," said he, "is especially full of warning to us; their progress seems to have been accelerated or retarded in exact proportion to the prevalence or absence of harmony among the artists themselves."

He made light of the difficulties which the new academy would have to face, saying that difficulties are the glory of genius, without which its energy and its brilliancy would pass unnoticed away, "like the electric fluid which flows unobserved along the smooth conductor, but when its course is thwarted then, and only then, bursts forth with splendor and astonishes by its power. Difficulties will yield to perseverance. The natural progress of taste in art is gradual; its advance is slow. It is through our Academy that the concentrated labors of the artists of the country can be brought to bear upon the public mind."

In this address Morse bemoaned the fact that the American artist, returning from the study of his profession in Europe, would find his own country unprepared to appreciate him. He showed Europe as a society where the artists and those that encourage them have proceeded onward together to a far advanced point in the March of taste, but that the Society of America had scarcely begun to move in the great procession. "The artist may go abroad," he said, "but he must not return."

Morse's picture of the American artist who, after cultivating his art in foreign countries, returns to find his own so far behind him in taste that he is doomed to starve in unmerited neglect, brought forth an indignant protest by an anonymous champion of the American Academy, who also took up Morse's objection to the intervention of any but professed artists in the management of academies. Morse was also taken to task for declaring that he thought it much better to employ living artists than to collect pictures by the old masters. He had quoted from one of Opie's lectures that "he who employs the humblest artist in the humblest way of history, contributes more to the advancement of National genius than he who imports a thousand chefs-d'oeuvre, the product of a foreign land.''

Morse's address created a furore in the world of art and precipitated a series of articles in the *North American Review*, in which he was attacked and defended with energy and sometimes bitter partisanship. Wielding a trenchant pen, he completely defeated his critics in a ten-thousand word reply and a heated polemic ensued, in the course of which the new members of the Academy of Design broke many lances with the defenders of the American Academy, not only in the *North American Review* but in the *Morning Courier* and the *Evening Post*. On the side of the National Academy were men like James Fenimore Cooper and William Cullen Bryant, the latter of whom was professor of Mythology and Ancient History at the National Academy.

Enmity grew between the two Academies and the campaign in the press assumed such proportions that in May, 1828, Morse, as President of the National Academy, and John Trumbull, as President of the American Academy, hurled printed denunciations at each other, Trumbull charging Morse with misrepresentation of the facts and Morse sticking to his guns and proving point by point that the American had tried to trick the artists and that the artists had refused to fall into the trap laid for them.

In Morse's final broadside to Colonel Trumbull, President of the American Academy, he defined the issue in the following words: "The National Academy is a real Academy for the promotion of the Arts of Design. Its plan was formed by artists on sound and proper principles. It is now three years since it was instituted and the artists are satisfied with its success. The institution has prospered beyond their most sanguine expectations. The American Academy of Fine Arts is not an Academy. It is only a sort of benefit club. The fundamental principle of its constitution is wrong, and the body of artists never could have united with it while they had a proper sense of their own character and rights. For many years the American Academy has been regarded with so much apathy that not one in ten of the stockholders attended its annual meetings. At the very meeting in which the plan of union with the artists was defeated, only about thirty, out of nearly three hundred, were present."

The establishment of the National Academy of Design marks the opening of a distinct era in the history of American Art. Year after year the artists comprising its membership re-elected Morse as President and continued him in that office even when he returned to Europe in 1829 to be gone three years. From 1827 to 1845 Morse presided over the destinies of the Academy and it is significant of the regard in which he was held by his fellow academicians that again in 1861, long after he had given up painting, he was again asked to become President and accepted for one term.

In 1841 the Academy had already proven its appreciation of Morse's service to the cause of Art by ordering his bust placed in the Council Chamber of the Academy and the fact that the Academy still gratefully remembers him, sixty-seven years after his influence in art matters had ceased to be felt, is evidenced by this memorial, the funds for which have been contributed by the members of the Academy and its distinguished President, Mr. Cass Gilbert, by whose presence we are honored.

It was in 1835 that Morse was appointed Professor of the Literature of the Arts of Design at New York University. He is a part of the history of this great educational institution and it is very fitting that Morse the artist and Morse the inventor should also be honored here as Morse the teacher.

It was in rooms assigned to him by the university in the building in Washington Square that the first chair of art ever established by any educational institution in the United States began to function. I had this in mind when in 1920 I suggested the revival of this chair of art to my good friend the late J. Sanford Saltus and, had not death removed him unexpectedly and prematurely, the Department of Fine Arts now happily in operation at the university, would bear the name of Professor Morse. Mr. Saltus had offered to contribute $75,000. of the $125,000. needed for the endowment of this chair and I had communicated this fact to Chancellor Brown.

The great disappointment of Morse's life was his failure to obtain the commission of the government for one of the four panels in the rotunda of the Capitol at Washington authorized by an act of Congress in 1837. Smarting under this rebuke, Morse sought to resign from the presidency of the National Academy, but his fellow academicians refused to hear of it. Thomas Cole, in a letter written to Morse under date of March 14, 1837, voiced the feelings of the artists in the following terms: "I have learned with mortification and disappointment," said he, "that your name was not among the chosen, and I have feared that you would carry into effect your resolution of abandoning the art and resigning the presidency of the Academy. I sincerely hope you will have reason to cast aside that resolution. To you our Academy owes its existence and present prosperity and if in after times it should become a great institution, your name will always be coupled with its greatness. But if you leave us, I very much fear that the fabric will crumble to pieces. You are the keystone of the arch; but if you remain with us, time may furnish the Academy with another block for the place. I hope my fears may be vain and that circumstances will conspire to induce you to remain our president."

The incident which cost Morse the loss of the commission for the rotunda of the Capitol was the publication of an anonymous letter in the New York *Evening Post* attacking John Quincy Adams, former President of the United States, for the introduction by him in Congress of a resolution opening the competition to foreign artists, as well as to Americans, on the ground that there were no artists in this country of sufficient talent properly to execute such monumental works. The indignant letter in the *Evening Post* was at once ascribed to Morse, who was known to wield a facile and fearless pen. Mr. Adams took great offense and, as a result, Morse's name was rejected and his great opportunity denied him. It was subsequently established that James Fenimore Cooper was the author of the anonymous letter and not Morse.

The artists could not let this affront to Morse pass unchallenged, however, and, at a meeting called by General Thomas S. Cummings, one of the founders of the National Academy, they subscribed $3,000. and formed a society which they called "a joint stock association of artists for procuring Morse to paint an historical picture." When they waited upon him in a body and made known to him the form they had decided to give to this public vindication of his talent, Morse was greatly moved, and at once was lifted from the depths of depression to a feeling of great professional pride at the thought that his peers had taken this unprecedented step for the rehabilitation of his fame. Morse accepted with gratitude, and it was decided that the painting could proceed. Morse insisted that it be painted not of small size as requested, but of the exact size of the panels in the Capitol Rotunda.

Morse's time was so much taken up by his telegraph inventions, however, that it seriously interfered with the painting and, writing from New York University under date of March 15, 1838, he asked General Cummings that no further payments be made to him on account of the picture until his return from Europe, when he would inform the Committee as to whether or not he could go on with the painting. The letter is worth quoting as it shows that Morse, even during the most feverish period of his labors attendant upon the launching of his invention, cherished the hope of an early return to the practice of his profession. The letter is as follows:

"Dear Sir: Circumstances relating to the telegraph, invented by me in 1832, will require my attention for an indefinite time, and I am about to visit Europe principally in reference to matters connected with this invention. At the same time, indeed, I have in view some studies connected with the picture which the association have commissioned me to paint for them. Yet I ought not to conceal from the gentlemen who have so generously formed the association, that circumstances may arise in relation to the telegraph which may make it a paramount duty to myself and my country to suspend, for a season, the commission with which they have honored me.

In this state of suspense, I have to request that no further collection of the installments be made until my return from Europe in the autumn, at which time I shall doubtless have it in my power to acquaint you with the course which it may be thought advisable to pursue. If possible, I wish as soon as practicable, to relieve myself of the cares of the telegraph that I may have my time to devote, more stenuously than ever, to the execution of my picture, and the benefit of the Academy and of the Arts.

With sincere esteem,

Truly your friend and servant,

Samuel F. B. Morse."

Later, Morse, finding that he did not have the time to execute the painting, returned to the stockholders the amount which they had subscribed, in full, with interest.

His success in the field of science never quite compensated him for his disappointment in the field of art. In a letter written in 1849 to his friend Fenimore Cooper, he says: "Alas, the very name of pictures produces a sadness of heart I cannot describe. Painting has been a smiling mistress to many, but she has been a cruel jilt to me. I did not abandon her, she abandoned me. I sometimes indulge a vague dream that I may paint again."

In 1864, when seventy-three years old, he writes, "I have many yearnings towards painting and sculpture, but I find that I can no longer place confidence in my eyes. I have made the sacrifice of my profession to establish an invention which is doing mankind a great service. I pursued it long enough to found an institution which I trust is to flourish long after I am gone, and be the means of educating a noble class of men in art to be an honor and praise to our beloved country."

In the life of Morse, written and compiled by his son, Edward Lind Morse, the author paints this picture:

"Wherever he went he had the faculty of inspiring respect and affection. An ever-widening circle of friends admitted him

to their intimacy, sought his advice and confided in him with
the perfect assurance of his ready sympathy. A favorite Biblical
quotation of his was 'Woe unto you when all men shall speak
well of you.' He deeply deplored the necessity of making enemies, but early in his career he became convinced that no man
could accomplish anything of value in this world without running counter either to the opinions of honest men, who were
as sincere as he, or to the self-seeking of the dishonest and un-
scrupulous.''

He has left behind him evidence of his skill as an
historical painter, as a portrait painter and as a
landscape artist, and his one and only venture in the
field of sculpture won for him a prize in London
when he was but twenty-two. Certainly his landscapes do not compare with those of his contemporaries, Asher B. Durand, Thomas Cole and
Thomas Doughty, but his portraits have character,
and those of DeWitt Clinton and Henry Clay in the
Metropolitan Museum of Art, to name but two out
of two dozen equally meritorious, show not only a
perfect technique but a fine sense of pose and composition.

Behind what a man does, there always stands out
the fact of what he is. There was not much novelty
or originality in his painting, only patient fault-
lessness, but it might well be said of him as a man,
what Thomson said of Congreve, he was:

"The unjealous friend of every rival worth,
Who gained no title and who lost no friend."

WILLIAM M. CHASE
Albion Polaseck, *Sculptor*

WILLIAM M. CHASE

I FEEL particularly happy today, as any man must in the moment when he has achieved a cherished and long-deferred ambition. All of you, no doubt, have wanted to do honor to William M. Chase, whom to know was to love. All of us, from sun to sun each day, are conscious of a good intention, but, alas! the sun sets each day with nothing done and sometimes even with the intention forgot.

I formed the intention to place the bust of Chase in this Pantheon of painters and sculptors, The Hall of Remembrance of New York University, a very short time after his death. Like a great many of you, however, I was engaged for a while in a more imperative work and while my intention never passed from me, by the very force of circumstances I had to defer putting it into execution.

As soon as I was out of my uniform, however, I at once set about realizing the project. My first impulse was to enlist cooperation of his fellow-artists and I approached several of them, J. Alden Weir, Blashfield, Paul Bartlett, Carroll Beckwith, Will Low, Daniel C. French, and received encouragement from all. Before definitely setting the machinery in motion, however, it came to me that in addition to being a great painter, Chase was a great teacher, probably the greatest teacher of painting America has as yet produced, and it occurred to me, knowing the character of the relations which always existed between this lovable and beloved mentor and guide and his pupils, that a much finer tribute would be paid him, if the bust which I proposed to enshrine here were presented by his pupils instead of by his *confrères* and fellow-artists.

I conferred with a number of these and with Mrs. Chase and the authorities of the university, and the plan was adopted by acclamation. Thus it is that the memorial to be unveiled here this afternoon is not only the lasting acknowledgment of a great painter's talent, but also a testimonial of love.

I take no undue credit for having pursued my intention until I made of it a reality. Alone, I could not have succeeded. It is to you, his grateful and remembering pupils, that the credit is due, for, if mine was the initiative, yours was the doing and the fashioning.

I shall not speak of William M. Chase as an artist, but rather as a teacher and as a man. I wish to speak of him in the terms that Carlyle used in speaking of Mirabeau: "the world," says Carlyle, "loves its original men, and can in no wise forget them, not till after a long while; sometimes not till after thousands of years. Forgetting them, what indeed should it remember?''

William M. Chase was an original man, not perhaps in the same sense as Mirabeau, who made as many enemies by his originality as he made friends, but in the sense that he made friends by a process that generally produces enemies, the process of saying what you think, regardless of the contrary opinion of the person you address, or who addresses you. Nothing was true for Chase because the verdict of the mob had decreed it. He had to convince himself by personal observation and study before he accepted any theory no matter how widely held. Even in contradiction, however, he had a way with him that disarmed, a gentleness, a sincerity, an evident desire not to wound, that melted all opposition and made resentment impossible. Again to quote Carlyle, ''the fact of all facts is . . . that a man be loved the better by men, the nearer they come to him.'' Mr. Chase was *so* loved by the men and women who came nearest to him, and these men and women were his pupils.

I will not go into his biography, nor discuss his merit as a painter. Others this afternoon will tell you that this aristocrat was born of humble parents, in modest circumstances. Others will tell you that his works hang in the Uffizi Palace in Florence and in the public galleries of New York, Boston, Chicago, Cincinnati, Detroit, Indianapolis, Philadelphia, Pittsburgh, St. Louis and Washington. They will tell you of fifteen medals and prizes awarded in this and other countries. I would like to say to you only that great as was William M. Chase as a painter, he was greater as a teacher and greatest as an "original man."

I knew him in my youth, when our relations were those of teacher and pupil, and I knew him later when it was my good fortune to commission him to paint the portrait of a number of my clients. He was a man of great dignity, who knew his value, and who liked to walk erect, at peace with himself and with his conscience. He could utter no unkindness, because his mind could conceive no meanness.

At the Art Students' League, where he taught for eighteen years, and later in his own schools here and at Shinnecock Hills, at Philadelphia, and at Carmel, California, he preached art as an interpretation of reality and turned out artists imbued with the idea that, to be a good painting, a picture must be suggestive, evocative and stimulating, and in addition be well done. By this he meant that artists are not born but made. He had no patience with cubism and fu-

turism and painting that dispenses with technique.
In an address delivered in 1916 at the annual dinner
of the American Federation of Arts he spoke of the
danger of the spontaneous theory in painting. "It is
a serious matter," he said, "when students are told
that they must not know anything in art and that
any indication in a work of art that the producer of
that work has had any training is proof of his failure." He was an original man, a painter of specula-
tive and scientific habit, a "persona sofistica" as
Vasari said of Botticelli, and the idea that a man
might be a "natural genius" and be able to paint
without long and painful study was too ridiculous
for him to discuss even.

He loved his work and took great pride in the
fact that he was a valiant soldier enlisted in defense
of the cause of Beauty and of Art. "I happen to be a
member of the most magnificent profession that the
world knows," he once said, and he lived up to this
conception of what a painter is by the most lofty
and the most rigid observance of every professional
principle.

I have met in some quarters the good-natured reproach that he was vain and pompous. To that
I need only quote what Ruskin wrote to a friend
who had asked him for an expression of what had

most influenced his life. "As for the things that have influenced me," wrote Ruskin, "I believe hard work, love of justice and beauty, good nature and great vanity have done all of me that was worth doing."

"Noblesse oblige," is a motto founded on vanity and so is the Japanese code of ethics, the Bushido of the Samurai, but such vanity inspires to high deeds and is to be admired and not censured or derided. To be conscious of one's worth is not a fault but rather a quality. It is only when the worth is fictitious that high self-esteem becomes a weakness. In Chase the worth was genuine and, therefore, the self-esteem was justified.

I shall not detain you longer. What I have said is what all of you believe and feel and it were idle to waste strength in battering down a door that is not even latched. I have wanted to lay a few flowers before the effigy of my old teacher and friend because he himself never lost an opportunity to give praise or encouragement when either was deserved or needed. He has gone, but before going he placed a posy before every shrine of beauty and gentleness and love that he encountered. Let us follow in his footsteps and live up to his teaching.

> "The world is wide with wonder now for me,
> Because of treasures that he bade me see,
> And every star flames newly bright
> Because I walked with him one night."